VACATIONS ON THE BLACK STAR LINE

We are not the same
I am a martian

—Lil Wayne

VACATIONS ON THE BLACK STAR LINE

Michael Cirelli

Hanging Loose Press
Brooklyn, New York

www.hangingloosepress.com

Printed in the United States of America
10 9 8 7 6 5 4 3 2 1

Hanging Loose Press thanks the Literature Program of New York State Council on the Arts for a grant in support of the publication of this book.

Cover art: "Secret Base," by Masakatsu Sashie
Cover design: Caitlin Meissner
Author Photo: Shaun "Scheme" Redwood

Grateful acknowledgment is made to the editors of the following publications and journals where these poems first appeared: *Voices in Italian Americana*: "Filet Mignon with Inspectah Deck," *Sixth Finch*: "Children's Story," *The Good Things About America* (Write Bloody, 2009): "B Boys Will B Boys" & "Upstarts In a Blowout," *Segue*: "T-Pain and the Robots," "T-Pain and the Fistfight" & "Up In the Treehouse," *Trespass Magazine*: "Black President" & "Can't Get No Betta'," *Flavorwire.com* & *LiveMag!*: "Michelle," *Hanging Loose*: "Brown Skin Lady" (for Sara) and "Brown Skin Lady" (The Smiths). The author would also like to thank the following friends for their steadfast support: Willie Perdomo, Rachel McKibbens, Christa Bell, Black Cracker, Erica Fabri, Bob Holman, Mahogany Browne, Nicole Sealey, Fish Vargas, Urban Word NYC and my family, among others. Excessive thanks to my meticulous editor Donna Brook, Hanging Loose Press, the dashing Bob Hershon, and Marie Carter. Sara, yatloml.

Library of Congress Cataloging-in-Publication Data available on request

ISBN 978-1-934909-20-1 (pbk)

Produced at The Print Center, Inc. 225 Varick St., New York, NY 10014, a non-profit facility for literary and arts-related publications. (212) 206-8465

for Sara, the bomb

Michael Cirelli, *Vacations on the Black Star Line* (Hanging Loose, 2010)

In this exciting new collection, "hip-hop poet" Michael Cirelli once again steps out onto the word plank, and dives into some rough seas. *Vacations on the Black Star Line* navigates the complexities of race and privilege through the lens of Mos Def and Talib Kweli's seminal "Black Star" album, named after the famed black nationalist Marcus Garvey's shipping line. Cirelli employs a range of styles and forms from signature narratives of a "white boy" living, loving and working within the Black community, to word portraits of R&B singer T-Pain and the movement of pitch-perfect robotics. No stranger to critical race dialogue, this young poet plows the ubiquitous terrain of whiteness through the eyes of a self-conscious anti-racist, longing for a culture to call his own. At times, that culture is "hip-hop" and at others it is:

> …herringbone gold chain
> hanging from the neck of a Tony Soprano
> devotee with dried marinara
> flaking from the hairs of his perfected goatee.
> Italy laughs at this version of Italian, of us,
> but I embrace it because it is something
> I can call my own.

In the poem "Definition," the poet outlines his family's bootstrap access to "the dream," but more pointedly follows up the poem with "RE: DEFinition," a new version that contains footnoted insights into many of the words in the previous poem. Under the term "My People," Cirelli acknowledges:

My People: *noun* No longer Italiano not even/Wop no longer Irish/Polack/no longer/in order/for the gears of race/to run.

Cirelli continuously echoes these sentiments throughout the collection, not just lamenting his own lost culture, but also caricaturing some of the tendencies that have contributed to its demise. In one of the many "Brown Skin Lady" poems, he wants to "call you *mine*." In another, he admits he feels "awkward like I had stolen one of theirs." These deliberate choices to incorporate oppressor language may seem brave, but Cirelli's intentions delve much deeper than merely outing white racism. In what seems the signature poem of the book, "Twice Inna Lifetime," the poet addresses his true obsession:

> I'm afraid this new intergalactic
> President of ours absolves my people,
> who live in West Oakland or Bedstuy
> like it offered us stripes, like it made us
> The Voyeurs of Inequity, like it added
> to our bios.

Always startling, at best these poems are a sucker punch right in the gut of white America. Vintage Cirelli word portraits, robot anthems, and homages to language and slanguage, pepper this second collection from the director of the award-winning youth literary arts organization, Urban Word NYC. In classic Cirelli fashion, the poems read as a complete story, a concept album: one that tries to reconcile his racialized, fetishized, exoticized and religified journey, while also recognizing his "tourist" status in the many communities he inhabits. *Vacations on the Black Star Line* is a bold, if not brazen, collection that contributes to the (much needed) dialogue about whiteness by way of honest, artful, thoughtfully crafted poems.

—Walt Whitman
Westhills, Long Island April, 2011

Table of Contents

III. Back to Black

IV. Still life with the roots

V. Ritual

VI. The Ecstatic

... few, if any, want to get their hands dirty these days, and it costs us. Consider, just for an example, the subject matter of race in America. Why hasn't racial anxiety, shame and hatred — such a large presence in American life — been more a theme in poetry by Caucasian-Americans? The answer might be that Empathy is profoundly inadequate as a strategy to some subjects. To really get at the subject of race, chances are, is going to require some unattractive, tricky self-expression, something adequate to the paradoxical complexities of privilege, shame and resentment. To speak in a voice equal to reality in this case will mean the loss of observer-immunity-status, will mean admitting that one is not on the sidelines of our racial realities, but actually in the tangled middle of them, in very personal ways. Nobody is going to look good. [1]

---

1   Hoagland, Tony. "Negative Capability." *The American Poetry Review* Mar/Apr 2003: Vol. 32, No. 2.

FILET MIGNON WITH INSPECTAH DECK

for Rich Villar & the Style Masters

Rich, your name means abundance, or Rich
it can mean what every year you stitch into it means,
or Rich can mean Purple, and for the sake of this
poem it does. I've already done things the way I do
the things I do, (wearing a birthday suit with spaghetti
stains). I need to pull the gold teeth from my poems!
Last week, I went to a panel discussion of pioneer
graffiti writers. They talked about *style* like it was bread.
T-KID borrowed a loaf from **CHAIN 3**, who gave props,
then made toast. **NOC** got the toast—treated it like the most
important thing since (sliced) bread—and made a BLT.
Thirty years later, a group of teenagers in Astoria craft
the BLT into a blowtorch. Still fire, still dough at its core.
Where I'm going with this, is that the steak needs to be rare,
Purple. The bread is best served fresh. Furthermore,
we'll have to toast with the robots, not forgetting
the poplars swinging outside the window.

I. New World Water

ASTRONOMY (8TH LIGHT)

Black like the planet/that they fear.

If those are stars, and what they make when they pepper
the sky, if it is a sky and not a road, is a shape we call
spoon, then the sky that is not a road might possibly be soup
or yogurt, but we call it a sky (and the spoon of stars
has its own name), and in that road of soup is a planet,
if it is a planet, and if what we call *planet* was assigned a color
that is feared in America, if this is America, and if fear meant:
"something *bad* might happen to you, so be on the lookout"
and "bad" had the same color of this planet in America
so the color called *bad* had to swallow the "bad," like a black hole,
had to make break/s, make tap, and scratch two records
together to fire/back, if what fire is is something that makes light,
and heat, so that the "bad" was no longer *bad* even when it was used
in speech like when he said "he is one bad mutha effer"
it was not *bad* meaning "bad" but *bad* meaning "good"—(like foot, like
hair, like skin)—then the skin that looks up to the moon,
as full as a record, reflects the light that shines off the sun that we call
the biggest star in the soup, and we see it down here in Fear,
where the people, if they are people and not spoons, bob their heads
to the light that shines from two mouths and is black.
The light from their mouths is black.

DEFINITION

Each morning
before school I would
sit at my parents'

diner with Dot,
whose smile shone
like an asterisk,

and we would eat pumpkin
muffins and stare out
the window

at the orange leaves
dancing on the hard edges
of the wind

or I would watch
my mother glide across
those off-white tiles

that spread across
the floor like a huge honey-
comb mosaic as she filled

the mugs of plumbers—
and I kissed her on the cheek
and skipped all the way

to Catholic school to learn
how my people got us here,
how they plowed through

the maize stalks down Broad Street
so that we could post a sign
that said "99¢ Breakfast Special"

and live the dream.

RE: DEFinition[2]

Each morning
before school I would
sit[3] at my parents'

diner with Dot,[4]
whose smile shone
like an asterisk,

and we would eat[5] pumpkin
muffins and stare out
the window

at the orange[6] leaves
dancing on the hard[7] edges
of the wind

or I would watch
my mother glide across
those off-white[8] tiles

---

2   DEFinition: *noun* What it all/means, or what the winners/write. The losers add/the footnotes/in blood.

3   Sit: *verb* An action that takes/away the burden of action,/or what my mother doesn't/do all day, so that her/ kids can do things/like this.

4   Dot: *proper noun* A star, or asterisk/in a constellation from across/Broad Street,/who ate her muffin in four quarters/like an American football game.

5   Eat: *verb* What Marie Antoinette/wanted her people/to do with cake.

6   Orange: *adjective* A color that could/or could not be/orange, and could/possibly be blue, or/Oglala.

7   Hard: *adjective* "Man"-like, or physics-like, or race-like, or life-like, or like the boyz in the hood, always.

8   Off-White: *adjective, noun, verb* When something is "off"/there's something wrong with it, when white is off/it has swallowed/all the colors of the spectrum,/off-white is like adding cream/to coffee except backwards.

that spread across
the floor like a huge honey-
comb mosaic as she filled

the mugs of plumbers[9]—
and I kissed her on the cheek
and skipped all the way

to Catholic[10] school to learn
how my people[11] got us here,
how they plowed through

the maize stalks down Broad Street
so that we could post a sign[12]
that said "99¢ Breakfast Special"

and live the dream.[13]

---

9   Plumber: *noun* A man who lays/pipe, raises girls, understands/bootstrap logic,
digging/holes, (not the privilege/of poeming about privilege)./Once in geometry class I told/
Brother Brennan that *my uncle's/a plumber he plums,* got two/nights detention for the outburst.
10   Catholic: *adjective, noun* Hurts so/good.
11   My People: *noun* No longer Italiano not even/Wop no longer Irish/Polack/no lon-
ger/in order/ for the gears of race/to run. (See also page 41).
12   Sign: *noun* An omen, marker,/token, symbol,/like when history repeated/and Neil
Armstrong/thrust one into the Moon.
13   The Dream: *verb* For the scientist: the predetermined movement/of robots; for
Martin: the undoing/of inequity; for "Other": the falling/and falling; for My People: the
cosmos's the limit.

re: RE: DEFinition

Whoa wha wha wha wha whoa whoa/O whoooaaa
whaooo whoa-oooo

Danny had the fake so when the doorman stamped his 16-year-old hand he'd book it to the alley behind Club Baby Head and press the top of his hand to the top of mine and then to Bri's then to Joe DiSanto's till we all had the stamp and could coat our tongues with Jäger and bounce our bodies off each other like bumper cars to Sonic Youth and I had oxblood Doc Martens wrapped around my ankles and my eyes pointed North until the blizzard caught up with me so I went to England singing *Meat Is Murder* and wore track suits and smoked pylons with Yardies and when I got back I met Danny at Snooker's and pulled girls with my new accent then left the next day for Vermont to give college another try but really ended up at Nectar's with the munchies eating gravy fries with Phish-heads and snowboarded with other bulletproof kids until Buddhism seemed a better pickup line so I hopped a bus to Berkeley and sold 12 elbows a day of hours to live in a monastery full of confused white people under the thumb of a Lama (I never met) and they were all either from Holland or Germany and they were not happy at all but they had money and they filled their meditation pillows with it like cotton and ran away from whatever money couldn't suture and I think I was 22 and I think I was high on cinnamon so I left again for Plum Village or Lodz toting a suitcase made of mesodermal tissue or Shreveport or 22 Muses or Oakland and then for LA to pour Fumé Blanc into sunglasses and then to Brooklyn where hip-hop is jacked electricity and beats broken and samples stolen so hip-hop (in a way) is white like me with all these stamps that resemble you because my stamp is your stamp and yours Jack or Terrance or Trugoy and yours and maybe you'll hear it in here: see its faint imprint on the back of my hand, this house where the doors are painted red and the hinges crafted from your black knuckles.

Children's Story

for Howl Sirowitz

Sitting on a blanket
embroidered with patches
beneath a column of bones
we listened to the poets
hold their penises
under the chestnut trees
and pretend poems can
be jazz but poems can never be
jazz, only jazz can be jazz.
My nephew Holden
liked Hal Sirowitz
best, Hal whose body is italicized
from Parkinson's, and who
tapped the microphone
like a cigarette,
and while he spoke
the Parks & Rec lady gave
Holden a free beach ball
as he struggled to pronounce
Hal's name, like his tongue
hadn't unlocked that sound yet,
so he insisted I was saying
a bad word Uncle Michael,
saying "Hell," and I said,
"no it's Haaal, Haaal Holden,
it's Hal," after which Holden
bent his mouth into that abstract
shape and said,
"Oh! Howl!"—as if he'd met
a hundred men named Howl
in his 6 years on this planet.

So we watched Howl Sirowitz
finish his poems, and I blew up
the beach ball, but Holden
scrunched his face into
a blowfish and gave me
the ball back. I asked him
what was wrong, and he told me,
          "You're in there Uncle Michael.
But I want to be in there."
So I opened the rubber cork
and I squeezed the ball flat, blowing
my kiss into my face until it was all-empty
of me—for Holden
to stamp his lips to the plastic,
and give that ball Life.

Brown Skin Lady

You an extra black white boy, Nicky said after I blurted bold
as blackmail that Tyreik only goes for *broke-down white girls* and that
made me feel so good so extra so black, while the white in me smiled
like a sickle like when Frank said, *I don't know what you are homie, but you ain't*
—white, as I made an illegal U-turn right in front of the Oakland PD,
and the boys from Richmond called me their n-word, and the kids at Manual
gave me dap, and I surrounded myself with all this darkness, packed my mouth
full of Shea butter & AAVE until I felt black in sheep's clothing,
which isn't black at all, but it comforted me to be so god damn down,
so schooled in hip-hop like hip-hop was a hall pass to blackness, and I even
dated black girls and got my fingers caught up in their thick dark curls,
or even better I grabbed onto a handful of dreadlocks and learned
that I wasn't nearly black as I thought because *you just don't do that shit.*

BROWN SKIN LADY

for Sara

I never looked at you like you were brown
skinned meaning you are not black, meaning
your tongue can wrap around America
like a scarf as you curse at the television. I'm in
the kitchen trying to make lentils like yours
and it's so windy in Brooklyn that a tree branch
taps my window like out of a horror movie
(where the black guy always gets killed first).
The TV shows the dirt where you were born from
smoking and little halos of dust remember
your first breath that doesn't look dangerous
even washed in bullets your mother doesn't look
dangerous and I picture you climbing some fruit tree
and yanking the most dangerous fig from it, for her.
You are the blackest of the black the most hated
most dangerous even now as the branch outside
my kitchen window is shaped like your name
in Arabic and reminds me who I eat daal with
who I wanna change the pronunciation of *god* for,
just so I can wrap a ring around your finger
and call you *mine.*

BROWN SKIN LADY

*If it's not love then it's the bomb, the bomb, the bomb, the bomb,
the bomb, the bomb, the bomb that will bring us together.*
                                        —The Smiths, "Ask"

If you cut someone off
from their culture they
will die. My lady
can trace her long finger
like a terra cotta branch
through history's rich
cemeteries and arrive at
The Prophet. There is no
separation of church
and state when your homeland
is called: The Islamic
Republic of Pakistan.
Where I'm from, we pretend
that god stays out
of our taxes, and that culture
is the alchemy that turns
blood white.
I am multiple selves
but I am white. I contain
multitudes but am still white.
American culture is distinguished
by whether you are born of
old money, new money, or
no money. I can trace
my lineage back to my first loan.
My family tree grows from a safe.
It seems "the most
dangerous nation in the world"
has it right. All the ammo

we drop over there, and the Muslims
are not dead, as I polish off
another eggplant parm. At the airport,
they study my lady's passport
and wonder where she has hidden
the bomb, and I want to tell
them, she doesn't hide the bomb,
she is the bomb.

BROWN SKIN LADY

Black Star was playing at the Justice League
in San Francisco, and like most hip-hop shows
the crowd was slathered in testosterone—so many
goons dressed in so much camouflage I felt like
I was camping in Vermont—and these guys rolled
trees into stiff branches, and blew the smoke from
their mouths up into their nostrils (which I could
never do), and I was with my black girl (actually
she was half-black-half-Jewish, a Jewbian)
and all eyes were on us, because she was so thick
it was like someone added cornstarch to her,
and the song "Brown Skin Lady" didn't help,
because that song always made me feel awkward
like I had stolen one of theirs, as all the black
and Latino people fanned the air with their fists,
so proud of having *skin the inspiration for cocoa butter*,
while my skin inspired tanning beds, inspired Scotch
tape: for all the brothers to look straight through me
at the *sellout* on my arm.

Brown Skin Lady

...or the one about how your Ami
would bring a strawberry
to your bed in the morning to get you
up for school, or she'd slide under
the covers and run her cold feet
on your warm piggies (which definitely
are not piggies in your family),
or the change of clothes ducking
in your backpack, or every "friend"
who came over who was more-
than-a-friend, and I like the little girl
ones best: the big knife that you sliced
a crescent off your 4th birthday
cake with, or zipping around
your backyard wearing a homemade skirt
and knees darker than
the rest of you while your grandma
watched from the kitchen stirring brown
skin condiments—because chutney
is brown skinned/lentils is ancient black-brown
irises/or red ones/or yellow like chunks
of moon—and you were climbing her
fruit trees: plum, lemon,
guava, pomegranate and loquat (all brown
skinned imported post-colonized
strains), or the ones about the whole family
at the beach (all covered) and looking
like a scene out of *The Namesake* except
Pakistani, which is why I cry so hard
during that movie, or my favorite:
at the airport in Houston,
little immigrant girl walks up to
a tall black man with a right angle on his
head and asks, *Are you Big Daddy Kane?*

B BOYS WILL B BOYS

Their fingers bend and twist like leaves in the wind.
—Reynold Martin

We used to bang our chests, and scratch
our pits, for territory. Do elaborate dances
that made us look 6-armed, or serpent-faced,
or meant *don't fuck with me, or you'll be in*
my peanut stew tonight. Some of us erected wood
forts and chirped *mine mine mine mine,*
then entrusted lead to the skull of anyone
who disagreed. Others thrust God into saw-grass.
Or made limbs puzzle pieces. Words like *Blood*
translate to *Safety* for some, as a mound of teens
grab their crotches like handfuls of barley—
Now we even bang for thoughts. Add a ™
to a fresh phrase, or a © to an equation in blue pills
that can cork my anxiety in forty minutes
or less. But I long for simple arithmetic.
Days when I would break dance with my "homies"
(on blocks too far to smell Ma's American Chop Suey
simmering on the stove), then get chased
all the way home—through driveways and 'cross
blurred intersections—till I reached the wild rhubarb
that grew along the back fence of my yard, and I'd jump
over it head first, to safety.

K.O.S. (DETERMINATION)

Maybe it was in the math—the long division
of building & destroying—or maybe it was how
letters/simple As & Bs & Ms & Cs could open like
an oyster, or that the number 7 on his jersey
had significance beyond luck, or the night
he and Eric drove his bucket to the LI Sound
and noticed how the sharp shank of moon
could cut through any teenage bullshit, because
William was only 16 years old when he memorized
the 120 lessons that weren't part of Wyandanch High's
curriculum, while most sophomores were trying
to grow goatees, or fretting over Homecoming, or
learning where this newborn musk between the thighs
could lead them—and William was busy separating the hard-
ware in a sentence, reworking the internal combustion
of language, *thinking of a master plan*, emerging Rakim Allah.

Hater Players

If you advocate Beelzebub
If you cosign red onions
If you say *I don't mean to be an asshole but…*
If you warm beer and dick jokes
Then green calamari to you! You need inside-out eyes…
If you doubt it
If you clock it up and down, every tick of heel to pavement
If you rotten ginkgo and self importance
If you not down Not
Feeling it
Then most likely you Stink Face most
Likely thieve in the day thief in the night
Likely lonely
Likely skurd
If you *don't understand why they trippin' if you ask me*
If you frontin'
If you all in my grill
If ya push venom from your subwoofer
If you boycott The Big Man on the top floor
Wearing a foam #1 finger
If you sour milk
If you bitter, you banter, you quicker bicker-er
Then you lack Buhloone Mindstate
Lack Makaveli
Lack-a-wanna Blues
Then you a horse sound + "sayer"
You dry of most high
(Because god is Booming!)
If you call the kettle black
If you stinging nettle anthropomorphized
If you wish you would
Then you a hater, playa.

Respiration

Anxiety is so First World.
—Michael Cirelli

I can feel the city breathing
down my back, I say to my therapist
as I sip green tea, and roll
a Cross pen through my fingers,
wearing soft leather shoes, soft
as caramel on my feet, and the deepest
blue trench coat hangs from my chair
like a wave and *if it ain't one thing,*
it's another, I complain
to the woman with bone-white
hair I pay by the ½-hour in a building
made of onions. Outside, there are enough
oranges to pave Broadway
with rinds. If we rounded up every exotic
coffee bean, we could line the sidewalks
with them like slippery marbles.
There is enough gasoline blazing
through the limbs of these taxis to melt
Alaska back to obscurity and I have this fisherman's
knot in my stomach *all the time* I tell her
but *there is medication for that* she responds
while picking ants from her fingernails.
If we stacked all the beef in this city
on top of itself like a sacred burial
ground, people in Poughkeepsie could smell
where we live—so *it gets harder and harder*
to breathe I say *especially when I'm underground.*
I search the street for grains of salt
that once added up/might plummet me
south of this threshold

as the new moon flashes its blade like a doctor's
smile—and I go up the leg of a tall glass
building like fizz rising, peel off the camel hair,
unknot, unlatch, unzip
everything cotton, silk and leather.

YO YEAH

after Josh Healey

Yo grandma
Break out the oil
The vinegar

Yo rewind
Bring that back—
Start this poem
With 108 *yos*[14] like a rap

Better yet scratch that[15]
Let's begin with 360 affirmations & head nods[16]

---

14   yo yo yo yo yo yo yo yo yo yoyoyoyo yoyo yo yo yo yoyoyoyoyoyoyoyo yoyo yo
yo yo yo yo yo yo yo yo yoyoyoyoyo yo yo yo yo yoyo yoyoyo yoyo yo yo yo yo yo yo
yo yo yo yo yoyoyoyoyoyoyo yo yo yo yo yo yoyo yo yo yo yo yo yo yoyo yoyo yoyoyo yo yo
yoyoyoyoyo yo yo yoyo yo yoyoyo yo

15   ~~yo yo yo yo yo yo yo yo yo yoyoyoyo yoyo yo yo yo yoyoyoyoyoyoyoyo yoyo yo~~
~~yo yo yo yo yo yo yo yo yo yoyoyoyoyo yo yo yo yo yoyo yoyoyo yoyo yo yo yo yo yo yo~~
~~yo yo yo yo yoyoyoyoyoyoyo yo yo yo yo yo yoyo yo yo yo yo yo yo yoyo yoyo yoyoyo yo yo~~
~~yoyoyoyoyo yo yo yoyo yo yoyoyo yo~~

16   yeah yeahyeah yes yesyeah yeah yeah yeahyesyesyeah yeahyeahyeah yesyesyeah-
yeahyeah yeah yes yes yeah yeah yeah yeah yesyesyeah yeahyeah yeahyesyes yeah yeahyeahyeah
yesyesyeahyeahyeah yeah yes yes yeah yeah yeahyeah yesyesyeah yeahyeahyeah yesyesyeah yeah-
yeahyeah yes yes yeah yeah yeah yeah yes yesyeah yeahyeah yeahyesyes yeah yeah yeah yeahyesyes
yeah yeahyeah yeahyesyesyeah yeahyeahyeahyes yesyeah yeah yeahyeah yesyesyeah yeahyeah
yeahyesyes yeah yeah yeah yeah yesyesyeah yeahyeah yeahyesyes yeah yeahyeah yeahyesyes yeah
yeah yeahyeah yesyes yeah yeahyeahyeahyes yesyeah yeahyeah yeahyesyes yeah yeahyeahyeahye-
syes yeah yeahyeah yeahyesyesyeah yeahyeah yeahyesyes yeah yeah yeah yeahyesyes yeah yeah-
yeah yeahyesyes yeah yeah yeah yeah yesyes yeah yeah yeahyeah yesyesyeah yeah yeah yeahyes
yesyeah yeahyeahyeah yesyes yeah yeah yeah yeahyesyesyeah yeah yeahyeahyesyes yeah yeah
yeah yeah yesyesyeah yeahyeah yeahyesyes yeah yeahyeahyeah yesyesyeah yeah yeah yeahyesyes
yeah yeah yeahyeahyes yesyeah yeahyeah yeahyesyes yeah yeah yeah yeahyes yes yeah yeahyeah
yeahyes yes yeah yeahyeahyeah yes yes yeah yeahyeahyeah yesyes yeah yeahyeah yeahyesyes
yeah yeahyeah yeahyesyesyeah yeah yeahyeah yesyesyeah yeah yeahyeahyes yesyeah yeahyeah
yeahyesyesyeah yeah yeah yeahyesyes yeah yeahyeah yeahyesyesyeah yeah yeahyeah yesyes yeah
yeahyeah yeahyes yesyeah yeah yeah yeahyesyesyeah yeahyeah yeahyes yes yeah yeah yeahyeahye-
syesyeah yeah yeahyeahyes yesyeah yeahyeah yeahyesyes yeah yeahyeahyeahyeahyesyes yeah

Now:

Yo grandma
Break out the oil
The vinegar

Yo ma
Let me take your order
Yo dad we'll be golfing
On Mars (watch the sand traps)

Yo Martian learn me how
To say *god* in Martian

Yo multiple literacies
Come wrap
Your mouth around
My ear so I can listen
To the ocean in there

Yo Rhode Island
Yo Mt. Pleasant Cranston Narragansett
Yo everyplace

Yo johnnycakes!

Yo Face
You look closer to *Oy*
Than to *Yo* with that beard and nose

Yo is I, and I am him—

Yo privilege I always spell you
Wrong/Yo right when can I do you? Yo
Wrong, in the eye
Of the beholder, get glasses

Yo you muggin' me

You know I'm muggin' back

Yo Spock
I'm so future
I got my appendix removed/Yo Mork
I'm so future
I only talk in 160 character
Texts

Yo talk to me
Until the pencil
In your throat splinters cuz
In the future, first will go the yeahs[17]
And last will go the yos[18]—

Yo Peggy McIntosh Jen Weiss Audre Lorde
Yo Sara Yo Freire did it work?

Will it.

---

17   yeah yeahyeah yes yesyeah yeah yeah yeahyesyesyeah yeahyeahyeah yesyesyeah=
yeahyeah yeah yes yes yeah yeah yeah yeah yesyesyeah yeahyeah yeahyesyes yeah yeahyeahyeah
yesyesyeahyeahyeah yeah yes yes yeah yeah yeahyeah yesyesyeah yeahyeahyeah yesyesyeah
yeahyeahyeah yes yes yeah yeah yeah yeah yes yesyeah yeahyeah yeahyesyes yeah yeah yeah
yeahyesyes yeah yeahyeah yeahyesyesyeah yeahyeahyeahyes yesyeah yeah yeahyeah yesyesyeah
yeahyeah yeahyesyes yeah yeah yeah yeah yesyesyeah yeahyeah yeahyesyes yeah yeahyeah
yeahyesyes yeah yeah yeahyeah yesyes yeah yeahyeahyeahyes yesyeah yeahyeah yeahyesyes
yeah yeahyeahyeahyesyes yeah yeahyeah yeahyesyesyeah yeahyeah yeahyesyes yeah yeah yeah
yeahyesyes yeah yeahyeah yeahyesyes yeah yeah yeah yeah yesyes yeah yeah yeahyeah yesye=
syeah yeah yeah yeahyes yesyeah yeahyeahyeah yesyes yeah yeah yeah yeahyesyesyeah yeah
yeahyeahyesyes yeah yeah yeah yeah yesyesyeah yeahyeah yeahyesyes yeah yeahyeahyeah ye=
syesyeah yeah yeah yeahyesyes yeah yeah yeahyeahyes yesyeah yeahyeah yeahyesyes yeah yeah
yeah yeahyes yes yeah yeahyeah yeahyes yes yeah yeahyeahyeah yes yes yeah yeahyeahyeah
yesyes yeah yeahyeah yeahyesyes yeah yeahyeah yeahyesyesyeah yeah yeahyeah yesyesyeah yeah
yeahyeahyes yesyeah yeahyeah yeahyesyesyeah yeah yeah yeahyesyes yeah yeahyeah yeahyesye=
syeah yeah yeahyeah yesyes yeah yeahyeah yeahyes yesyeah yeah yeah yeahyesyesyeah yeahyeah
yeahyes yes yeah yeah yeahyeahyesyesyeah yeah yeahyeahyes yesyeah yeahyeah yeahyesyes yeah
yeahyeahyeahyesyes yeah
18   yo yo yo yo yo yo yo yo yo yoyoyoyo yoyo yo yo yo yoyoyoyoyoyoyoyo yoyo yo
yo yo yo yo yo yo yo yo yo yoyoyoyoyo yo yo yo yo yoyo yoyoyo yoyo yo yo yo yo yo yo yo
yo yo yo yoyoyoyoyoyoyo yo yo yo yo yo yoyo yo yo yo yo yo yo yoyo yoyo yoyoyo yo yo
yoyoyoyoyo yo yo yoyo yo yoyoyo yo

Yo X the theater in Harlem
Went silent as a dead cricket
When you went Omawole

YOmawole!
Yolele!

Yo haters, hi

Yo pain, and lies and Truth's
Coming out party
For the thing that
Made my world mimic
A sleeping bat

I wanna walk from that place
Where night comes
For 6 months straight
And stand at the edge of light
Scruff and hungry
As the sun appears
For the first time
Squinting.

Yeah.

THIEVES IN THE NIGHT

He wore a pirate ship, wore diamonds on the keel of his shoes, and if wind was Everything, if wind was bonbons, was the Password to the City, was truffles or oil drums that could be stacked up and shown off to the president, then his sails were ready for the filling—So when they accused him of biting their style, he looked up from his dinner plate and replied, *that's all I've ever known.*

TWICE INNA LIFETIME

for Christa Bell

1. *When I Consider the Caucasian-American*

As a kid, I used to hang over
the hull of this boat and look straight
down, my face full of wind like a flag,
and the water looked like the moon.
And as we glided across the surface
of the moon and Providence sprang up
like an extraterrestrial space camp
the deeper and deeper we penetrated
Narragansett Bay, I had no fear of getting
closer to the edge, wanting to run ashore
and greet the aliens with my capgun.
Back then, the only Black I knew
was the color of the Boston Bruin's jersey
and I loved the way Gord Kluzak
threw a punch. I've only felt "other" twice
in this lifetime, the details are not relevant,
but the moon is. And even on the moon,
I still somehow believed I belonged,
wearing oblivion on my face like melanin
paint on the hull of a spaceship—

2. *My People*

I'm afraid this new intergalactic
President of ours absolves my people,
who live in West Oakland or Bedstuy
like it offered us stripes, like it made us
The Voyeurs of Inequity, like it added

to our bios. My cousins live in Providence
where every wanna-be-thug-gangsta-
goomba hangs a lynched Jesus from his neck,
and the wardrobe of African-America
off his ass. I don't know who's worse off.
In Brooklyn, my friends with privilege
have the privilege of understanding
privilege. We pay off student loans
from our Adventures in Ethnography.
We read culturally relevant books
from other cultures and swathe our tongues
in hip logic, cupboards full of organic beans.
So quick to say *fuck it*
when the blame finger is pointed bull's eye—

3. *Reflection Eternal in the Manner of a White Boy*

I put a mirror
in front
of me and fix
one to the wall
behind me, stand
in between them
and look at my image
go on and on and on.
I am large.

4. *Poem in the Manner of a Satellite*

Moon, your skin
Is so good.
Moon soft morph
Silk moon spun
Hydrogenated oil.
Moon so alive.
Moon with good
Skin, I envy.
Sun, overrated star.

Sun, ego-star.
My 20/20 space goggles
See millions of your
Brothers, engines that
Mimic god's intestine.
Pluto, Mars, Saturn,
I was given your names.
You Indians away
From India. You Columbia,
New England,
You can't dance no more.
We won't allow it.
I only read your books
In my binaries. My
Hard tongue.
But Moon, Moon so alive,
So soft a print in
You is immortalized.
Moon I can't keep
My eyes off.

5. *Vacations on the Black Star Line*

When I vacation on the moon,
the drinks are so cheap I can buy
a shot for everyone. When I vacation
on the moon, I've already learned
your curse words, already know how
to ask for everything. When I vacation
on the moon, I don't want to look like
a tourist. I've studied the architecture
of ribs, I know the history of each skull
step. When I look into the eyes
of the aliens, I know the pain they've seen.

II. Automatic

MAGIC IN A MORTAL MINUTE

for Amber

This minute has 2,700 seconds in it. I built
the scaffolding in my head while the subway car
hiccupped on its tracks all the way here/now.
I try to gift-wrap this idea with tree bark,
tie an electron around it—how one minute
can contain forty-five, or 102 years, or a whole
Plum Village (where all I remember is burning
my mouth off with Dijon mustard)? Yesterday
at the Museum of Natural History, I spent 72 minutes
with my little sister. We walked around a spiral orb
that was a simile for Time & Space. Each step took us
346 million miles and when she peered through
a giant telescope, the starlight that glinted
in her young eyes traveled 4.1 billion years just to die
right there. *It was well worth the trip*, I thought.

T-Pain and the Robots

*"Robot voices" became a recurring element in popular music
during the late twentieth century.*

Most days he would just stare
into the red reflectors of his toy robot's
eyes until he got dizzy. At breakfast,
he would pretend his Cocoa Puffs
were meteors floating in the Milky Way.
At night, he'd sneak into the kitchen,
steal the aluminum foil,
and wrap it around his arms and legs.
He painted his Little League helmet silver.
Built an interplanetary army
out of old spark plugs and mufflers he lifted
from the auto body's dumpster.
In the summer, when his mom brought
out the fan to shoo away those sticky Tallahassee
nights, young Faheem would sing straight
into the whorl of blades for hours.

POEM IN THE MANNER OF A REFRIGERATOR

to be read through a vocoder or with Auto-Tune

My song goes:
Refrigerator, Refrigerator,
Refrigerator, Automatic Automatic—
I can hold that note
All night long. I can hold that note
Till the power slips and my insides
Melt. Tonight, I'm the master of cold.
Tonight, I dream of singing
Backup. (A cool cat with a top hat.)
Forget the grapes in their fur
Overcoats. Forget wanting to scream
Through my compressor:
Take out the takeout! Take out the takeout!
Automatic, Automatic—
But Hunger just awoke from a bird's nest.
Hunger has hot breath, not like
Mine, mine like toothpaste
Commercials, mine like
York Peppermint Patty.
Hunger stands there in his pj's, squinting
At the light inside my chest. This little light
So fascinating to his kid. His kid
Who opens and closes me
Like a cigarette box, trying to catch
Me dark. What's the fascination
With Light?
With Fire? Hunger only cares
About warmth.
Overlooks the value of cool.
Doesn't appreciate how I hold my note

Summer after Summer:
Refrigerator, Refrigerator,
Refrigerator, Automatic Automatic—
Everyone talks about Fire as lifesaver.
What about Ice? I make Ice.
I keep Ice, Ice.

UP IN THE TREEHOUSE

There was a time when skinny
dipping was feasible,
when it was perfectly fine
to drop drawers and swim naked
in a stream off the Kancamagus
as a troop of Brownies crossed
the wooden bridge. I was too young
to know "the big deal" till a few years
later when one of us got a hold
of Playboy's fluffy tail
and we had to build a treehouse
for those magazines to perch on
in plastic bags like goldfish—
and this was the beginning
of *getting into things*
like going down to the boatyard
in the winter where the boats
were hibernating on cinderblocks
dreaming of fire hydrants
and we'd break into those boats
and let the brown liquids in crystalline
decanters burn our tongues
or we'd steal knives and machetes
and big metal fishing hooks
(that must have been severed pirates'
hands), and for some reason we buried
them behind my *mema's* house
hoping that they would grow
into the sharp warriors of our dreams.

T-Pain and the Fistfight

The boys picked on his song, caught
him in moon boots smuggling a shooting star.
If women could squeeze a hard-jelly-bounce
into their chests, slide a chemical slug
into the top lip, then Faheem wanted the vocal
cords of a spaceship. He wanted to sing
like the Jetsons' housekeeper as she polished
her ray gun. He wanted a smile
like a pencil sharpener. But the taunting
cut deeper each day, so Faheem recycled
six bags of cans & bottles, and bought
brass knuckles for a punch like a robot's.
His aluminum baseball bat was his lightsaber.
He was only eight, too young to know
about comas. Too young to register losses.
When they finally pried the bat from his
sequin-gloved hand, there were still four bullies
standing, and they beat asteroids into his
blue-black face. They beat him until his lip
opened like a thundercloud, and bled ball bearings
all over the outfield.

THE ALCOHOLIC ROBOT

Every day after work at the Secret
Service, he can be found at Q's Tavern.
This morning, he sifted through a garbage
can that smelled like sulfur. After lunch,
he unwrapped a birthday gift someone forgot
on a park bench. His circuits are a metaphor
of nerves—and he needs a drink.
Candy pours on Tuesdays at Q's. He likes
the bartender. All of them. If you sit next
to him, he wants to buy you *a drank*.
If his metal jaw, or his eight-digit hand mis-
fires on your knee, he blames it on the alcohol.
If you refuse him, the booze is rubber,
and if not, screws. Most nights you will find
him beeping at the end of the bar, ecstatic,
plugged into the socket by the jukebox
like a cell phone. Every song that plays
is a sad one: earthlings tumbling down the machine's
shiny hardware, the robots in love.

T-Pain's First Job: JD's Electronics & Appliance Superstore

Faheem filled out the application, three times.
We don't hire people under 18, they said.
We need daytime help, the manager told him.
But young Faheem was persistent, stalking
the aisles of equalizers, noting the nuances
of tweeters. He knew the coolest air conditioners,
he knew which robotic arm could spin a whisk
fastest—could burst egg whites into clouds.
Each refrigerator had its own song.
As did the stereos: Pink Floyd mimed a robo-
tenor from 27" speakers and Faheem nearly
spilled onto the red linoleum! When he finally
got the job, he could be found among the right
angles of television sets, all playing *Star Wars*
from VHS recorders. He marveled at how
something so black and shiny could father Luke.

III. Back to Black

TRAPPED IN THE CLOSET (CHAPTER 1)

Shit think, shit think, shit quick,/put me in the closet

It's 7 AM. The sunlight is amplified by the bedroom window, and Sylvester is the ant awoken by it, tangled in sheets that aren't his, that feel like sand/paper, on Mars. It all comes back: da club, the Planet of Ass that each shot of Patron nourished like the Sun, the crashing his Cadillac straight into mattress. Next thing: she's morning breath, she's cheap wig, he's coat & keys, he's *Should I go?* logic with no question. He'd dive from that 5th-floor window if not for the pedigree of his shoes. But he can't go, can't exit because hubby just got home. (Where was he last night, who knows?[19])—From inside the closet, the slats of the door hyphenate Sylvester's face in shadows. He watches the outcome change hands on the bed still dank with him, but hubby can smell the dank: hubby's about to let the cat out the closet, about to snort the trail of funk to its master. The husband swings open the shower curtain/he angles his head like an ostrich beneath the bed/he looks in the dresser? for, a gnome?/he walks up to the closet/he goes up to the closet/now he's at the closet/*damn he's opening the closet closet closet*—Lucky for Sylvester, sly Sylvester, he's got his bang apparatus cocked, he's got cold steel in the moment of chaos, his Beretta shining like a mirror reflecting sweat—and it's pointed straight at the pastor, Rufus.

---

19   See "Trapped (Chapter 2)" for a clue.

ANECDOTE OF 16 BARS

"Jezus Christo's horny twin"
placed a jar in the Bronx
near Sedgewick Avenue.

It had a red tongue in it
similar to the one found years
earlier south of the Mason-Dixon

somewhere between St. Louis
and the Delta. The only difference
was that the previous jar's tongue was blue.

There have been others—one colored
thunder that Presley stole from Berry,
not to mention the jar with a clicking tongue.

That one was very very old. But the Bronx
jar was the one we were waiting for.
It was the sound of black troubadours.

The projects rose up around it and were
no longer wilderness to those who hadn't
lived there. Teenagers across the heartland

romanticized the bravado of Bronx, wanted
a lick of the red tongue, to fit into its baggy jeans.
This is the age when *the word* became fresh

and it took dominion everywhere.

BLACK PRESIDENT[44]

In 1926, the sci-fi novel *O*
*Presidente Negro** dreamed the year
2228 black. Black as the middle
of my eye. In 2263, Bruce Willis
flies a cab that zooms across the silver
screen, and Deebo is prez.
In another movie, a rogue comet
is hurtling through the cosmos like
an errant free throw, as we spray
our spaceships with synthetic melanin.
Look to Morgan Freeman, fresh out
of Shawshank, to save us—
When destruction is closer than the knife
blade on our throat, in a future
where we forgot how to walk, only
then have we imagined a black president.
In 2008, the poster on my wall
has a 4-letter word and a black face,
who is not an athlete, not a rapper.
I put black on a pedestal. Pray to black
five times a day. I make black the new
white. Today, America is the absence
of light. We walked into a time
machine, and pulled down the lever
hoping to hit the blackpot. Swallowed
November's time capsule, shaped like
an *0*, like an aspirin, and waited by
our televisions, that don't project

---

44   *My president is Black/In fact, he's half white/So even in a racist's mind/He's half right*
                                                                    —Jay-Z

holograms, in living rooms that dream of
being silicon. It's not the future
but it is—my car doesn't fly—but a black
man (with Pain woven into his moniker)
belts a robot lullaby through my amplifier.

*O Presidente Negro (The Black President) was published in 1926 by Brazilian author Monteiro
Lobato: he imagines the 2228 U.S. presidential election between the white male incumbent,
a white female feminist, and the cultivated and brilliant leader of the "Black Association."

MISOGYNY

trumps Racism—
        not because of the ease

a black man can say *bitch*—
but because so many whites

(like me) can spin that word
        like a revolver's cask
                can unmask it, dilute it

in so many ways—dress it in bow tie,
taps, face painted black: *beeyotch, biznitch, biatch*

while we would never
        utter the word *n******.

WHITE BIRD

Tina is white, and Jewish, and near 60,
and made out of firecrackers.
Once a week, she lights her wick
and shoots straight up to the 21st floor
of Bellevue Hospital to teach poetry
to a group of teenagers who leak.
Patiently she plugs a hole here,
with clumps of rap lyrics, a crack there
with silly putty. Most of the poems
they write sound like Uranus, and some
like defibrillators. The ones that scream
for attention say things like,
I scratch my ass. And after I scratch my ass
I smell my fingers. Today at the reading,
the girl with the itch wanted more shine
than time allowed and Tina had to say *no.*
The girl called Tina a *bitch, a fuckin' white bird,*
fuckin' bird, white bird over and over as security
dragged her from the room. Tina continued
the reading calmly, as the bird calls got fainter
down the hallway. Instead of a firecracker,
I realized that Tina is a white bird, a bouquet
of feathers that tells the wind which direction
to lift her.

PHIFE DAWG GETS A KIDNEY

and his mother is happy
as a clam, better yet
a clam in high water,
the most practical time
for a clam to be happy
when the tide is high
and those bivalve mollusks
are free from their predator's
grasp, free from clams casino
jackpots—from being
unhinged from their seashells
by the seashore in a world
that over-metaphors.
She sits in a chair between
the two hospital beds,
like sitting upon the throne
of a wave, and watches
her son and his wife sleep.
This past summer, in between
dialysis sessions, Phife surveyed
thousands of fans with one
simple question, *Can I kick it?*
Looking at him, skinny as a fin,
I thought of buckets, buckets like
mouths filled with sand
or sad clams, and I responded
No you can't—
This morning in Los Angeles,
lying in the bed next to him
with her eyes closed, a smile
spread across her face wide as
a pitch-black mussel,
Phife's wife dreamed of the ocean.
She is not a metaphor.
She is his perfect match.

MICHELLE

She answered the door
in a simple red dress,
her hair folded into a tight
spool—Barack wanted to grip
the polished rung
of her collarbone and climb
into her mouth, but this was
their first date, so they hotboxed
his blue Jetta until the smoke
was so thick it could be spread
onto shortcake, and he promised
her adjectives like *interesting*
and *audacious*, and he rolled
another jay, not wanting
to come 'cross no square brother
at the firm,
and Michelle liked the way
his words were pennies flicked
into a fountain, and finally
they checked out a Spike Lee joint,
and after the movie he fit
his hand into hers all the way
home where he sealed his lips
to her ear and promised
      an obelisk for her garden.

IV. STILL LIFE WITH THE ROOTS

WALKING ON THE MOON

This is how it
happened: how I
got so cool
I could write poems
in the manner
of refrigerators, how I can
identify the muscle
in a rhyme scheme—
because Santa dr-ropped
some hip-hop
into my stocking, because Dad
dropped me off
to see bands with names
like Throwing Muses or Jane's Addiction
and said "have fun"
and I did—which got me
into knee-high Doc Martens
and I wore them
to Catholic school,
got me around Krishnas
who gave me magazines
filled with blue aliens
blue, blue aliens with red pulses
on their foreheads,
with six arms!—and because
my parents didn't flinch
at that (or maybe it was
a clandestine flinch because I was
still an All-Star, still had As
straight as braced teeth,
still had blonde hair
and Doug Flutie eyes),
I could renounce meat,

I could leave college after a year
and go kiss girls in England
under an iron bridge, I could
move to a Buddhist monastery
and make prayer wheels,
or get mindful
in France, or guzzle vodka
in Polska, or unknot nooses
in Birmingham—because I
was still paying for school
(when I went),
because I worked hard
in restaurants like them,
and because I called every night
I could open their minds
to the world I stalked
in ways I'd never believe,
I could surround myself
with poems in San Francisco
where the Beats have pacemakers,
and surround myself with
monks with ears like satellite
dishes who spoke Vietnamese
like the enemy,
and surround myself with black
people, black people that
had space jive, had cosmic
language wrapped
around their fingers,
and I homaged those words
and deconstructed that swagger
and breathed into the phone
like it was oxygen
but it was really Mom and Dad
waiting home
holding their breath
as I boarded
every new rocket ship.

BIRTHPLACE

Deep in the Boogie Down—
      the bassinet of the boom bap
            where the trinity is The Treacherous Three,

English is the third language
      behind Bronx and Puerto Rican,
         and I was nervous

because I only speak Catholic school
      and I'm a Red Sox fan.

I'm just a student of KRS-1, not a son,

on a train fourteen stops beyond my comfort
      zone hiding behind headphones coughing
         bass, and a backpack full of lyrics:

Notorious B.I.G., Rakim, Perdomo,
Run DMC, Brooks, wanting to be real cool,

wanting to be their "dawg"—
      but feeling like a mailman,
         another Elvis

to the students I will lead
      through a workshop in a language

         I itch to get my rusted cavities around.

I am hip-hop.

You can blame Santa Claus,

who in 1986 in order to save sleigh
space, left Run DMC's *Raising Hell*

in the stockings of all the naughty kids
in the suburbs. Little did he know

his prank on white America would leave
parents up in arms forever.

In the same vein, their little angels
would also be throwing their hands in the air

and waving them carefree at role models
with cornrows from the Dirty South

on BET while sturdy women in thongs
"back that thang up" at Jones Beach.

Seventeen years later, I still haven't grown
into my parachutes or found the laces to my shell toes.

Mom's worried this "phase" may never end—

You can find me in the club, mimicking
camouflage, with a Larry Bird throwback jersey, mouthing

the words to "Player's Anthem" like I had game,
like I could relate to the hustle.

Nonetheless, I am still the dash in Jay-Z, the graph,
the clientele, the connoisseur who knows everywhere

I'll never be. I am the slovenly tongue popularized
by God's son, the white boy M1 wants to slap,

the Rock & Roll that's black, the breakbeat, the heart,
the movement, the art—

I claim nothing but hip-hop.
          I'm the white Eminem.

When the Puerto Rican chef at the restaurant I work in
told me I look "all NASCAR,"

I said, "No, I'm hip-hop."
          "Fur ril?" he said. "Yes, Pharrell," I said.

I actually lived in my grandma's basement for two years
while she roasted root vegetables upstairs. I'm underground.

I rocked Air Force Ones when they only came in the colors
of privilege or minority—when Sergio Valente pinstripes

were like a fresh sheet of paper. I'm old school.
My pops is incarcerated for pushing dope, the noun.

That makes me part gangsta. You know what time is it—

When I win the Pulitzer Prize, for Realness, the Nobel
for my translation of Hip-Hop, I will step to the stage

and represent Rhode Island to the fullest, shout out God
"first and foremost, without whom none of this would be possible,"

the rotund wrapper with an alabaster beard
who gave me my first Run DMC tape.

This is dedicated to you.

TAWK

You know, when you talk,
but if you're from where I'm from
you may be "tawking,"
and depending on who you're
tawking to, and where they're from:
which bend of road
or angle of sun or moon-
light hits the dark room
of throat, informs
the way they say what they say,
which side of lip
the words plummet from or how tongue
strings 'em together chops
'em screws 'em,
how Mona is from a below
place where the speakers
speak like they're pulling up
word anchors from the deepest
depths of Mouf, or in some parts
more salt, and others more peppa:
whether cayenne or corn—
I'm in love with a boy
from East Oakland whose word is
stretched longer than
twelve hearses,
and his Dickies are starched.
In Texas, it is the vibration of
the dinner bell, in Kansas
something different.
In New Yawk, Nueva Yol,
Brooklawn-Vietnawm,
where the tongues pulse like
marquees, talk keeps the lights on!

When T-Pain dissected
the tone of Flux
Capacitor, of E.T.'s grand
piano, and named his album
Rappa Ternt Sanga, he wasn't being
ignorant, or ignant at that, wasn't bad
at spelling (maybe bad
at rapping which is why
he turned singer), but he was
accounting for the texture of the dirt
in his teef. He was showing it off
in his smile. This makes sense to me.
Because I want everyone
to see the Rhode Island in my elbow.
I want everyone to know
I was born in a kawfee mug
floating down Narragansett Bay
and raised by a Lion.
And by kawfee mug I mean:
I was born in an alphabet that left its R
on the dressa—and by Narragansett Bay
I mean: an estuary flowing with wrenches
and ratchets and uniforms—and by Lion:
I mean my mother, who's been serving
breakfast to regulars since 1975
(when I showed up),
and to this day they still come to see
her, my ma
who tawks to each and every one
of them cuz she's *gotta hotta-gold*.

Upstarts In a Blowout

It's 4AM and my little sister is blow drying
her hair, straightening the mother
tongue out of it. She took the bus down
last night, by herself. This morning
the latest knock-off-Beatles perform
a free concert for America's wakeup show.
My sister is batty over Nick. Each band
member has a sharp name like Nick, or Jo
or Kev(in). My sister is washed in their image.
Has their pink ears plastered all over the walls
of her bedroom. When we get to the park,
every teenager has calculated the opening
of Nick, or Jo, or Kev's lips. If only the obsession
was literature, or ice hockey, or paper
shrines to Paul Robeson. I let go
of my sister's hand like unclipping
a leash, and watch her rush the 10,000 faces
that look just like hers. On a side street
I see the band being shuffled from Vegas
on wheels. Nick's face has a deep fold across it
like someone is about to make an origami
duckling out of it. I say, *Nicky, You've come too far
to blow out now*—On stage, the TV man aims 42
light beams at their puffy heads. Their chins
start to melt. My sister screams from the front row
catching every drop in her mouth.

WORD.

It has been said
    that when the cosmic plumber

laid pipe in a Tigris
out poured the word, and the word was *all good.*

Eventually the word grew a shitty diaper, and from
that tipsy tongue dribbled first words: either *Ma,* or *No!*

As children our words are well used in song.
In elementary we love the combinations of letters
    that make words whole.

In high school we give our words big bony elbows
so they take up as much space as possible.
Through college we ask *How many words?*

More words more problems, some might say—
words like *commitment, chemotherapy, culprit.*

Words can fail us, words like *goodbye, never, pulpit.*
But I am sprung

    on the word. Sometimes I lie in wet cement
just to be close to it. I rub my face all over the keyboard

to know its touch. It feels like the syllables
that make glass shiver from too much bass.

Like a ring of men with proper nouns stamped into flesh.
It feels fresh. This is when the word is best,

    when *Word.* means *Yes!*

V. Ritual

WITH ME IN MIND

The priest said, *do this in memory of me*,
and the sissy boys rang a bell back
and forth gayly, and I was too young
to walk the line so I watched as Fr. McNally
pressed *play* on each tongue, but no music
came out. Instead, the parishioners bolted
their lips tight and let Jesus melt down
their throats like a sugar cube salvation. I knelt
among the cannibals, on my filthy knees,
one "Our Father" away from forgiveness,
with a caterpillar cupped in my praying hands,
and peeked down the pew at Amy Hogg
in her painfully plaid skirt,
wondering if she even knew my name.

CROSSING BROOKLYN BRIDGE

for Holden and Piper

Last year Holden was everything *astronaut*, so we wore
aluminum foil halos as we ascended the most famous space
bridge in the world—and my wingtips were moon boots
and his Chucks were anti-gravity Chucks—and we slid up
the cables like reverse fire station poles. This year, *Spiderman*
has crawled between the five-year-old's ears, and he claims
the bridge's cables are a web spun by his blood-orange hero.
His ten-year-old sister still walks behind as unimpressed
as last year, when we walked across the air over a river, our
Summer Ritual. Her glasses dipping down her smart nose,
she has her eyes set on the distant continent: Canal Street.
When we get there, back alleys bloom handbags and watches,
but she is more interested in the Buddha statues. She tells me
I'm a Buddhist, and Holden chimes in *I'm a Ninja!*
At the Vietnamese restaurant, The Buddhist orders *pho*
with raw beef (*pho bo tai*), I get the tofu & Chinese mushrooms,
—and Holden tells me that my mushrooms are *baby spiders*.

BROOKLYN PERSONIFIED

for Mahogany Browne

All the poems the kids write personify
Brooklyn. Hips: bricks. Bones: brown/stones.
Brooklyn is a Caribbean woman, with Wonder
Wheel doorknockers, pushing a white baby
in an eight-hundred-dollar stroller. Brooklyn
wears an apron, a kufi, a red & black lumberjack,
makes the best pizza, patties, bagels, hip-hop.
But I want to de-animate Brooklyn. Want her legs
to turn back into Eastern Parkway & Atlantic.
Want her bloodstream to resign to Q, G, F trains.
I want her voice that is not a voice to rewind into
the barrel of a gun, the horn of a dollar van,
the busted speaker dangling from the ear
of a mosque. I want Brooklyn to open her arms
and give me a parking space, a sunny apartment,
a noisy block with kids playing in the blast
of water from a fire hydrant.

"Post-Race?"

On 137th St., a Mexican
woman sells tamales
from a yellow cart
and my Los Angelino girlfriend
loves tamales, but the tamales
she loves are pronounced
with a T and an H, with a hint
of a D in there
and those are the *thdamalez*
she wants. I suspect those
are the ones this *Meh-HE-con-Ah*
sells. See, we're the type of "post-
race" couple that loves fresh
wok-a-moe-lay (like it was a Chinese
dish), or that try at the very least
to trill an R, and we always add
an extra R like our tongue
was a card in a bicycle spoke,
spoken too long.
I never know how to feel about this.
How I feel about wedging an H
between the soft wings of Angeles,
or censoring the J in fajita (although
fageeta sounds ridiculous).
It's a beautiful thing to try, but how
pretty is the crash landing?
What do I call where they are protesting
today in Iran, Eh-rdan, Eye-Ran,
Ee-Run? How many pennies
at the bottom of the well
intentioned? It's because America
is half-assed that I ask these questions.
My people speak General Tso,

speak Chalupa, speak Chicken Tetrazzini.
Being a good American I know
most about food. I even know that
traditionally, the masa in tamales
is made with lard, which is a no-no
for my honey. In English she tries to
ask the woman who hears in Spanish
if her tamales are made with pork fat.
They struggle back and forth with different
metaphors for words that neither of them
knew, until finally I break the quagmire
with, *La masa tiene lardo?*, (surprising them
both)—and the Mexicana responds
si, to my lady's *oh no!*

ARS POETICA

When they came to New York City,
with their difficult names—strings
of D-Js or M-Bs—that my tongue loses footing
on, I wonder if I was as much the ass-
hole I am now, standing on the sidewalk
taking pictures of the damage, or if
I was ever a conduit to the myth
that stages buildings to the heavens, or a shot
at constellations, before the Department
of Everything set in, and the streets became
jammed with us, in our shiny black cars as shiny
as a crocodile's eye, not wanting to give up
a nose hair. I wonder how white was I
when we crashed, or if the news had reached
Africa long before they wrapped up
The Dream in batik robes
and crip-walked across the Atlantic
like ionized Conquistadores. Most likely
I was all-the-way-Gringo antes del touchdown
on Ellis Island-Jamaica-Queens, and I
was searching for bombs in their luggage
and I was humming Springsteen poems and I was
not the welcome they'd expected, not
the pineapple, not the garland of Benjamins
to be draped around the neck, I was more like
the silk rope. How long did it take to become African-
American? How long before the dazzletronics
of our Republic rusted? How long until
your kids got vaporized by Technicolor,
and when did their hands turn to fang
in your pocket?
Can I clarify something?
I am more than John Wayne Coca

Cola smiles more than Saltines and deviled eggs
and a cross strapped to a dagger more
than the inbred cousin of Kentucky bluegrass and fried
chicken and that is not me on the sign,
not my grandfather or my penniless benefactor
regardless of the Space Jam Jordans on my feet.
I am a hybrid of everything bleached from
my motherland(s), and whether you know
it or not, my parents still burn the oil
in their elbows seven-days-a-week.
I am herringbone gold chain
hanging from the neck of a Tony Soprano
devotee with dried marinara
flaking from the hairs of his perfected goatee.
Italy laughs at this version of Italian, of us,
but I embrace it because it is something
I can call my own.
For five years I built my savings
and bought a used Saab story, and a week
into this new mobility, two African men
pulled their banged-up Astro van, packed
to the roof with strollers, out of a parking space
and into my car, and it was like my body
got hit, like my fender was my face
and I was bleeding rubber, cursing these
apologetic Africans with 6s, and 13s, grabbing
for any bit of info that would send
them back home, which was the Bronx I learned.
This is where it gets tricky:
Reflected in Mbaye's eyes, who was rubbing the dent
like a belly, were my two eyes blue
as anti-freeze, looking at Djibo offering
to fix the car in three days, to keep it off the books,
(*he's learned fast* I thought).
They both see me Colonel Sanders see me Oscar
Meyer Madoff me Border Patrol me Me me Michael
Jackson and you think I see you Curtis Jackson
see you OJ see you Oscar Grant see

you Menace to Society you NWA you Doughboy,
when all I really see is the side of my car
crinkled like an aluminum foil hockey puck.
But we live in America now, where one wrong turn
can Cypress-shadow everything good you've ever
done, can taint you *bad*, not bad meaning good
but bad meaning bad. You know how
there's two sides to every story but you're too
bludgeoned to tell yours? You know how it's easier
sometimes to swallow mouthfuls of red
dirt than to speak? Than to call bullshit. You know
how sometimes you just wanna dump a fifth of gasoline
into the throat and be all the way bad. Be Judas kiss
gone wild Platinum. Be Limbaugh on crank.
But for now, I'll just continue with my quiet good.
The good no one hears but god. I'll continue to wait
in the half-light of blame, and drink coffee from paper
Chinese cups with these two men, and they were
still sorry, and I had eased up too, learning
they'd been in New York longer than me,
and they had cousins in Connecticut,
and Illinois, and San Jose, their family spread
all across this country like a highway, their kids
attending Catholic school. They were official African-
Americans, and I felt bad that I had been so
angry, that I could just turn a switch in my mouth
and shine the beast in any direction I wanted.
Eventually the po-po came, the police who knew
who was wrong before I even opened my lips,
and as Djibo and I handed our registration and insurance
over to the officers, they asked us who was at fault,
and like good Americans, we pointed at each other and replied, *him.*

CAN'T GET NO BETTA'

If I'd of known better, I would have kept
the Bible on its shelf, but anger got the best
of me and I ripped up that good book again.
Tiny words and phrases blanket my apart-
ment so that everything looks mislabeled as I
tour jeté out the door, and my better half hollers,
good luck finding someone better!—and she may be
right. On the subway, I size up every mannequin,
looking for better booty, better medulla.
At the gym, I pedal the stationary bike to a better
place, like wherever dead people go, but end
up no better than when I started. I take a shower
with men who have better bodies than mine,
but not better minds. I go to a diner that claims
"the best coffee in NYC," but it doesn't taste
any better than any other coffee in NYC.
In my notebook, I try to find a better way to say this.
The better person might have just let it go, offered
a bucket of roses and been done with it, but there
is something about my god that is wrathful, that
not only sharpens the teeth of each word but also
puts poison on the tips. A god that doesn't know
any better, and by god I mean me.

ISLAND

I'm jumping out
the window
with this one.
I'm unleashing
a noose
off the side
of Walt's bridge.
Ejecting from
the cock-
pit may be
better, so as to not
domino the fam.
Only if a landing—

An island.

God there though,
(*Masha'Allah*), in flip
flops, dragging
a rake through
the sands of
my defects of
character like
a Zen garden
for the righteous.
Scary here, stranded
among the coconuts.
Furthermore, only
get to take one album,
Stakes Is High.

BECOMING MORE HUMAN

> *Dehumanization, which marks not only those whose*
> *humanity has been stolen, but also (though in different*
> *ways) those who have stolen it, is a distortion of the*
> *vocation of becoming more fully human.*
> —Paulo Freire, *Pedagogy of the Oppressed*

For someone like T-Pain it would
mean extracting the robotics from the larynx,
or for vampires, they might try substituting
coffee for blood, or lemonade
for blood—a Michael Jordan, or Phelps,
would need to start smoking cigarettes
like cigarettes was bananas
or bran muffins,
which suggests that they are beyond
human, überhuman, and need to slink
back down to our level of humanity,
or maybe they are the most human,
filling up the limits of their humanness like
a gas tank, which implies limits to humanness
and undermines, say, the Buddha,
who sat under the Bodhi tree for 49 days
until he shook off the human dilemma,
or Jesus, who proved superhuman when
he moonwalked on water, and they did
these things for us, so we could be good
to each other, which is to say that being more human
is being more good and if that is the case
then I'd just have to copy my Nana.
But maybe becoming more human
is less about being good
and more about being real and the hip-hop
adage of "keeping it real" has it right

and all the rap superheroes, with their flamboyant
chains, have always known how to become more
human (except for the gold teeth
because gold teeth isn't human), but I regret
keeping it real sometimes because
sometimes keeping it really, really real
has caused me more trouble than it was worth
and made me feel like shit, not human—
When Paulo Freire talks about becoming more
human, he approaches it from the back side
of the mirror, like if we do less of becoming less
human, then we become more human, which might
mean taking on more *I'm sorrys,* or incorporating
more *Thank yous* into our slang, or we'd have
to share more make more room for everyone else,
which might be hard for Pilgrims, hard for folks
who want to give less. Or for someone
like me it might mean applying lotion to my tongue,
or a padlock, it might mean making everyone relevant
other than the Planet I. For someone like you
it might mean making *you* more relevant, could be
as simple as looking into the front side of the mirror
and seeing someone good, even if you
are a monster, a crook, even if you are
Frankenstein, who would have to unscrew all the bolts
in his body — but then he might fall apart —
which may be just the thing to do
to become more human.

VI. THE ECSTATIC

BISMILLAH

If ever the fight in us
breaks us, and we can't
press down on the pump
and blow Life back
into this, if instead we push
down and it all blows up—
because the same mechanism
that pumps air, also detonates
bombs—then I promise you
I will still convert, if not
to get under your skin like
a blood blister, then surely to get
as close to black (as the soil
under God's finger nail)
that my skin will allow,
to watch my beard spider down
my chest and be kin
with more prayer than food,
with trenches hollow as crescents,
so that I know what it feels like
to submit my palms
to the ground in His name
with a gun pointed
at the back of my head.

Notes

All of the poems in the section "**New World Water**" are titled, and in the order of, the songs on the album *Mos Def & Talib Kweli are Black Star*, except the addition of "re: RE: DEFinition" and four extra "Brown Skin Lady" poems. Except where noted, all epigraphs in this section are from the lyrics of the song being remixed in its poem. "New World Water" is also a song on Mos Def's *Black on Both Sides* album.

"Astronomy (8th Light)": *"Make break/s"* is referring to the break beat which birthed hip-hop music, as well as Curtis Blow's "The Breaks," and in the spelling invokes the one-man show by Marc Bamuthi Joseph, "The break/s: a mixtape for stage." *"Bad meaning bad but bad meaning good"* is sampled from Run DMC's "Peter Piper."

"RE: DEFinition": The reference to *"boyz in the hood"* being hard is from N.W.A.'s "Boyz in the Hood."

"re: RE: DEFinition": *Meat Is Murder* is an album by The Smiths. "Jack or Terrance or Trugoy" refers to Jack Gilbert, Terrance Hayes and Trugoy of De La Soul.

"Brown Skin Lady": AAVE is the acronym for African-American Vernacular English.

"Hater Players": *"I don't understand why they trippin' if you ask me"* is a line from Kanye West on the remix of Beyonce's "Ego." *Buhloone Mindstate* is an album by De La Soul. *Lackawanna Blues*, originally a play written by Ruben Santiago-Hudson, was adapted into the film directed by Loretta Greco. Makaveli was a stage name of the late Tupac Amaru Shakur.

"Yo Yeah": *"Yo is I, and I am him"* samples Snoop Dogg, as well as Jay-Z. *"You muggin' me/You know I'm muggin' back"* samples Lil Wayne's "Always Strapped." This poem also name drops educators, activists, and poets. Peep game.

"Twice Inna Lifetime": *"When I Consider the Caucasian-American"* references Terrance Hayes's poem "Woofer," and the use of *"hip logic"* also alludes to Hayes's collection with the same title. *"Reflection Eternal"* refers to the hip-hop duo of Talib Kweli and DJ Hi-Tek.

Several poems in the sections "**Automatic**" and "**Back to Black**" borrow titles from songs on Cody Chesnutt's *The Headphone Masterpiece* album. The poems are:

"Magic in a Mortal Minute," "Up In the Treehouse," "Michelle," "Upstarts In a Blowout," "With Me in Mind," and "Can't Get No Betta'."

"T-Pain and the Robots": The epigraph is taken from Wikipedia. Faheem is the birth name of T-Pain.

"The Alcoholic Robot": This poem references these T-Pain songs: "Bartender," "Buy U a Drank (Shawty Snappin');" and "Blame It On the Alcohol" (Jamie Foxx featuring T-Pain).

"Trapped in the Closet (Chapter 1)": This poem is a retelling of the R. Kelly song, and the epigraph is from the song lyrics.

"Anecdote of 16 Bars": This poem is after the Wallace Stevens poem "Anecdote of the Jar," and the first line is sampled from rapper U.S.

"Black President": Along with the noted Lobato novel, this poem makes allusions to the movies *The Fifth Element*, *Deep Impact*, and *The Shawshank Redemption*.

"I am hip-hop.": "*Back that thang up*" is sampled from rapper Juvenile from the song "Back That Azz Up." "Player's Anthem" is a song by Notorious B.I.G. This poem contains various other references to emcees.

"Upstarts In a Blowout": "*You've come too far to blow out now*" is sampled from the Cody Chesnutt song that this poem is titled after.

"Phife Dawg Gets a Kidney": "*Can I kick it*" is quoted from the Tribe Called Quest song of the same name.

"Island": "*I'm jumping out the window with this one*" is sampled from Ron Brownz. "*Stakes Is High*" (by De La Soul) is my favorite album of all time.

The section "**The Ecstatic**" is titled after the Mos Def album of the same name.

MY RAY GUN WEIGHS A TON

Written and performed by Michael Cirelli
Produced by Black Cracker

To download the MP3 of this Auto-Tune poetry album visit:
http://myraygunweighsaton.blogspot.com

Track Listing:

1: Vacations on the Black Star Line

2: Filet Mignon with Inspectah Deck

3: T-Pain and the Robots

4: Song of the Refrigerator

5: I am hip-hop.

6: T-Pain and the Fistfight

7: T-Pain's First Job

8: The Alcoholic Robot

9: Island

10: Brooklyn Personified

11: Down with the King

12: Becoming More Human